Sleep Tight

Chimichanga

Written by: Samantha Lyn Walljasper

Illustrated by: Katie Reed

For my amazing husband, Dustin and children, Axton, Meika, Brantley, and especially Ryker… our youngest "Chimichanga Baby."

Every night my mommy wraps up my little brother in his tortilla swaddle just like a tiny, cozy burrito.

She puts him on his back in his warmer bassinet, and his closed eyes look like sweet, mini grains of rice.

Sleep tight chimichanga.

Sometimes he opens his eyes back up. He smiles and happily burps up a dollop of sour cream.

My mommy gets a paper towel and cleans him up. She wraps him back up like a cozy burrito and puts him back to bed. Sleep tight chimichanga.

He opens his eyes back up again, but he is not smiling this time. He begins to cry and spits up runny, white, queso cheese all over his sheets.

My mommy gets more paper towels, a handful of napkins, cleans him up, changes his sheets, wraps him back up like a cozy burrito, and puts him back to bed. Sleep tight chimichanga.

He opens his eyes back up again. He cries a little more and then lets out a little, juicy gas. My mommy checks his diaper and finds a very small, side order of refried beans.

She gets more handfuls of napkins, cleans him up, puts on a fresh diaper, wraps him back up like a cozy burrito, and puts him back to bed. Sleep tight chimichanga.

She gets a whole box of napkins, cleans him up, puts on another fresh diaper, wraps him back up like a cozy burrito, and puts him back to bed. Sleep tight chimichanga.

One Full Order Of Ground Beef

He opens his eyes back up again. He has a spot of salsa on his cheek and a fingernail that is slightly too long.

My mommy cleans his cheek, puts cream on his cut, clips his fingernails, wraps him back up like a cozy burrito, and puts him back to bed. Sleep tight chimichanga.

He opens his eyes back up again. He sneezes a clump of guacamole out of his miniature nose.

My mommy gets a few more napkins and his aspirator, sucks out his nose, cleans him up, wraps him back up like a cozy burrito, and puts him back to bed. Sleep tight chimichanga.

This time he doesn't open his eyes back up until morning. He has clean sheets, a fresh diaper, a comfortable tummy, soft cheeks, a clear nose, and is as warm and cozy as burritos can be.

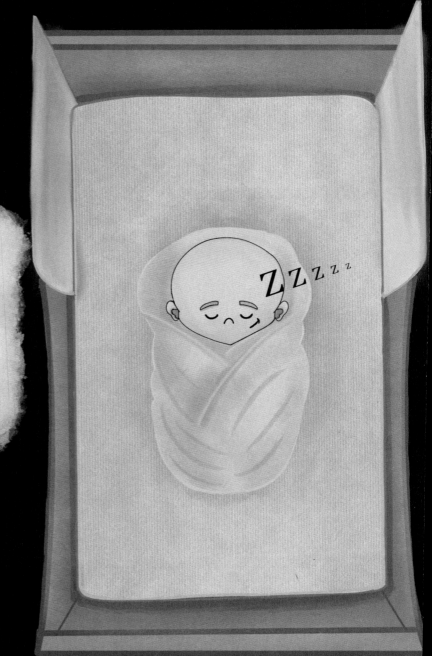

And good night chimichanga.